spot

BACKYARD ANIMALS

SNAKES

by Mari Schuh

AMICUS | AMICUS INK

tongue

fangs

Look for these words and pictures as you read.

mouth

skin

A snake hides.
Do you see it?

A snake is a reptile.
Some snakes are small and thin.
Others are big.

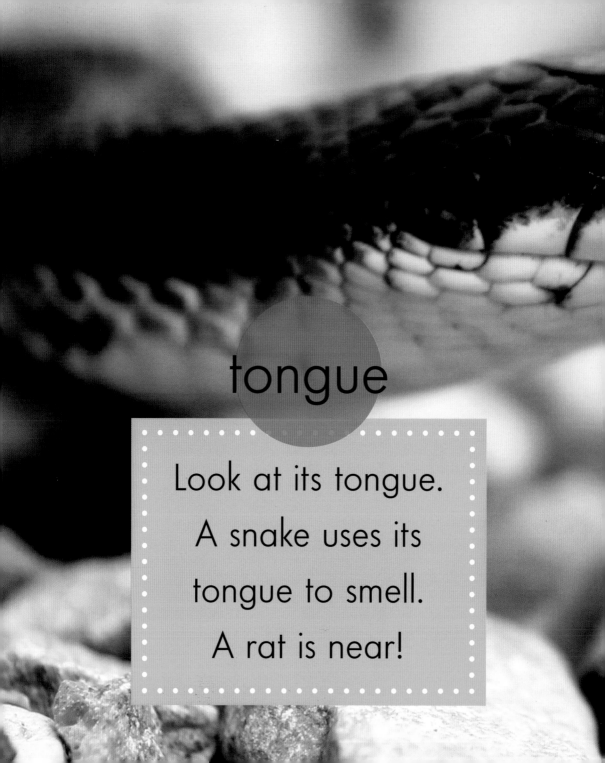

tongue

Look at its tongue.
A snake uses its
tongue to smell.
A rat is near!

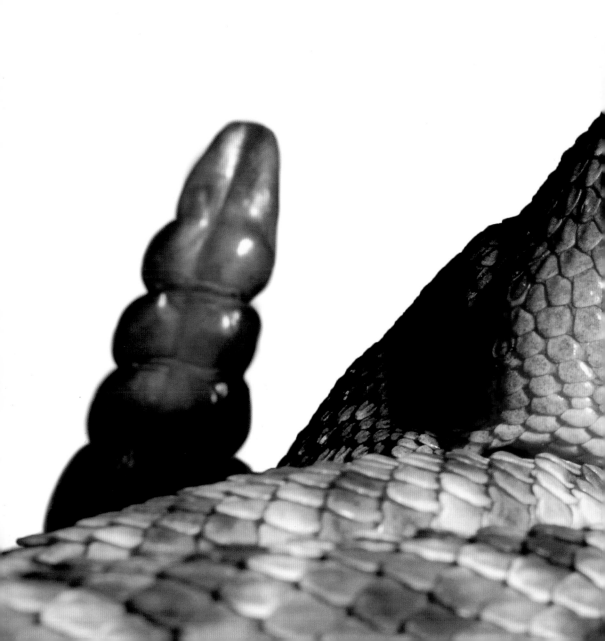

fangs

Look at its fangs.

They are sharp.

Fangs bite into animals.

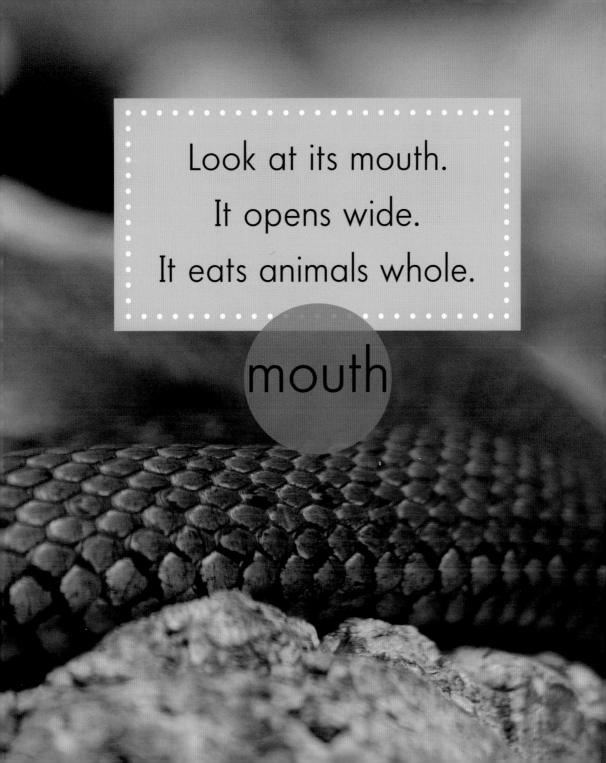

Look at its mouth.
It opens wide.
It eats animals whole.

mouth

skin

Look at its skin.
Snakes shed old skin.
This is called molting.

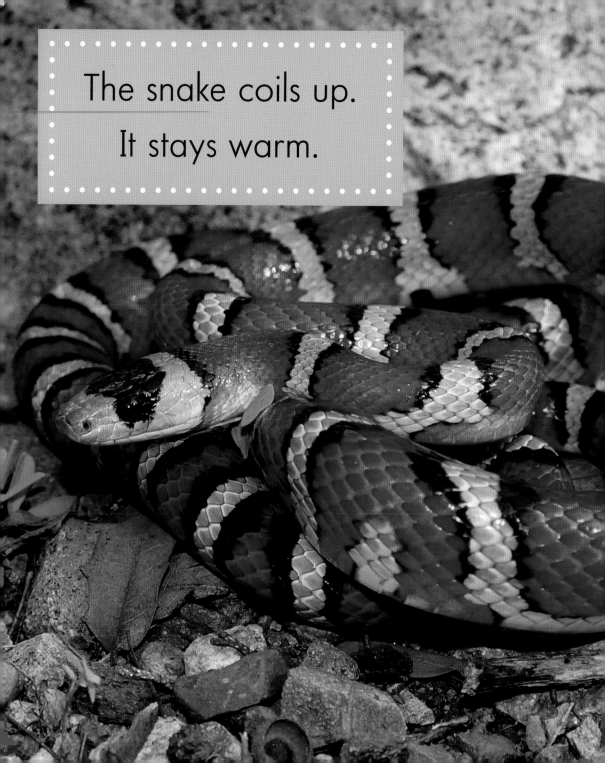

The snake coils up.
It stays warm.

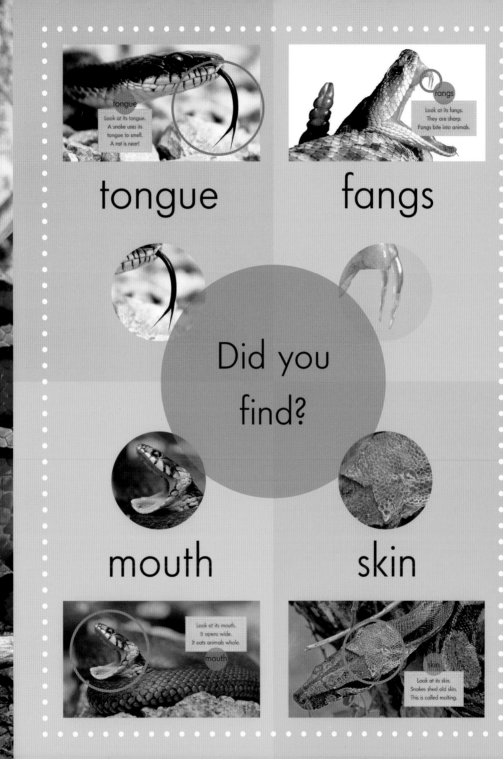

tongue

Look at its tongue.
A snake uses its
tongue to smell.
A rat is near!

fangs

Look at its fangs.
They are sharp.
Fangs bite into animals.

Did you find?

mouth

Look at its mouth.
It opens wide.
It eats animals whole.

skin

Look at its skin.
Snakes shed old skin.
This is called molting.

Spot is published by Amicus and Amicus Ink
P.O. Box 1329, Mankato, MN 56002
www.amicuspublishing.us

Library of Congress Cataloging-in-Publication Data
Names: Schuh, Mari C., 1975- author.
Title: Snakes / by Mari Schuh.
Description: Mankato, MN : Amicus/Amicus Ink, [2019] |
   Series: Spot. Backyard animals | Audience: K to grade 3.
Identifiers: LCCN 2017053729 (print) | LCCN 2017055838
   (ebook) | ISBN 9781681515878 (pdf) | ISBN
   9781681515496 (library binding) | ISBN 9781681523873
   (pbk.)
Subjects: LCSH: Snakes--Juvenile literature. | Vocabulary.
Classification: LCC QL666.O6 (ebook) | LCC QL666.O6
   S3868 2019 (print) | DDC 597.96--dc23
LC record available at https://lccn.loc.gov/2017053729

Printed in China

HC 10 9 8 7 6 5 4 3 2 1
PB   10 9 8 7 6 5 4 3 2 1

Mary Ellen Klukow, editor
Deb Miner, series designer
Kazuko Collins, book designer
Holly Young, photo researcher

Photos by Age Fotostock 10–11, 12–13;
Alamy 12–13; Getty 8-9; iStock cover, 1;
Shutterstock 3, 4, 4–5, 6–7, 14

SNAKES